Uncle Pazzo's <small>SHORT</small>

TALL
Tales

Uncle Pazzo's Short Tall Tales

Toem Publishing, Minami 9, 1-16, Chuo ku,
Sapporo, Japan 0640809

www.to-em.com

ISBN - 978-4-908152-05-4

Contents

Uncle Pazzo lived alone with his cat Moo, but he was always busy. His friends and family visited him A LOT. And why did they do this? Because he had a FANTASTIC garden with delicious bugs? Because his house was big and close to a volcano? Because he always had fresh apple pies waiting for his bear friends? No, no, and maybe.

People loved to visit him because he had a different hair-style every day, and because he told AMAZING stories. Children sat around his table, and he would tell them his stories.

After Uncle Pazzo told his stories, he asked them questions about the story, just to make sure they were listening. This book has 30 of his stories, with some questions to help you practice a very important skill...listening.

Uncle Pazzo reads the stories twice to his listeners. Sometimes, he pauses at the parts that are the answers to the questions. The first reading he does is slow. He occasionally asks his listeners if they understand a difficult word. He usually acts parts out when possible.

The second reading is done at a faster speed. If his listeners get all or most of the answers correct, they get some reward.

For Reo ,Remi, Rena, Haruki, and Yura

There are no stories without you.

Story 1

Greedy

Tom was a nice boy, but he had one problem:

He was very greedy. Greedy people want a

lot of things ALL THE TIME. If his mom gave

him 1 cookie, he wanted 5. If his friend had

a new pencil, Tom wanted a new pencil case and 10 new pencils. Greedy.

One day, Tom was shopping with his mom. The store's name was Yummi's, and there were a lot of candy and snacks in the store.

"Mom," said Tom, "I want those potato chips."

His mom told Tom to wait. "Mom," said Tom, "I want them now."

"Please wait," said Tom's mom again.

But Tom couldn't wait. He took the potato chips, opened the bag, and started to eat them.

His mom was mad, his mom was surprised, his mom looked around, and she saw a policeman.

Tom was eating the potato chips when the policeman walked up to him. "Hey, did you buy those chips?" the policeman asked Tom. The policeman looked angry.

"No, but my mom…" Tom looked around, but his mom was gone. The policeman took Tom's hand and brought him to the front door.

Tom's mom was waiting for him. "Don't," said the policeman, "be greedy."

The Girl and Her Cow

In a small city, there was a girl named Rena.

Rena's friend Remi liked Rena very very

very very very much. On Rena's birthday,

Remi asked her, "What do you want for your

birthday present?"

Rena thought about that for a long time.

'What do I want?' she thought. 'What do I need?' she wondered.

Finally, she knew what she wanted. She said, "I want a cow." So, on her birthday, Remi gave Rena a cow. The cow's name was **Boo**.

Rena loved ice cream. In the morning, Rena went to her cow. **Boo** was sitting in front of the TV. She was watching a baseball game.

She asked the cow, "Good morning **Boo**, can I have some ice cream?"

Boo looked at her and said, "I can give you milk, but I can't give you ice cream. My milk is warm, but ice cream is cold."

Rena sat down next to **Boo**. Then she called Remi. Rena asked Remi, "What can I do?" Remi gave Rena a good idea.

Rena went behind **Boo**, and pushed her

into a refrigerator. Now **Boo** lives in the refrigerator with her friends and family.

And Rena can eat ice cream anytime she wants.

Story 3
Fall

Summer was finished, and the weather was getting colder. The leaves on the trees were changing color: red and yellow and orange.

Suzi loved this season. Fall was her favourite time of the year. She liked to go outside and play in the leaves. She liked to make a big pile of colorful leaves, and then jump into it and throw the leaves all around. She did this all day.

One day, Suzi was about to go outside, but she saw snow on the ground. All of her leaves were under the snow.

But she didn't feel sad. Suzi changed her clothes, went outside, and made a big pile of snow. Then she fell into the snow and threw it all around.

Story 4

Always Late

One day, a boy named Tony was running to school. He was late. Almost everyday, Tony was late, so his teacher was always angry at him.

Tony was running very very very fast to school. He was running so fast that he didn't see a turtle on the stairs. Tony stepped on the turtle and fell down. "OOOOOOOOO-OUUUUUCCCCHHHHH!!!!!" Tony screamed. "AYAYAYAYAYAYAYAYAYAYAYA," the turtle shouted.

Tony looked at the turtle. It was an old turtle, and it wore glasses. Tony got up, and said, "Sorry Mr. Turtle, are you okay?" The turtle was angry.

It said, "No, I'm not okay. I don't like boys stepping on me. Be careful, and stop being late for school. Everyday you run to school. You are dangerous. Wake up early, or get an alarm clock." The turtle slowly walked away.

After school, Tony went shopping. He

went shopping for an alarm clock, and he was
never late for school again.

Story 5

Moon Boy

On a cold winter night, Sam and Bebe wanted

to climb a mountain. "Let's climb Mt. Pointy-

head," said Sam. "Ummm...that's the tallest

mountain I have ever seen...but okay, let's go," answered Bebe.

They walked and climbed and pulled and stretched until finally, they got to the top.

It was incredibly beautiful. The stars were shining bright, so close that Sam and Bebe reached out to touch them. But they weren't that close. The air was fresh and clean. And the moon looked bigger than 1 million soccer balls.

They were very quiet. Then, Sam whispered, "I wish I could live on the moon."

"Why?" asked Bebe. "Nobody lives on the moon. What would you do?"

Sam answered quickly, "Nothing. It's just so beautiful that I want to go. I would probably want to come back home."

"Good idea, moon boy," said Bebe, and they started to go back to their home.

Story 6

The Turtle and The Airport

Sara's house was very noisy. She lived next to
an airport, and she had 4 brothers and sisters.
Sara was the oldest. She was 10 years old. In
Sara's bedroom, there was a bird and a turtle.
The turtle was quieter than the bird, so she
liked her turtle very much.

One night, many airplanes were flying over
her home. She couldn't sleep. "I just want a

quiet home," she said to her turtle.

"I know a quiet place," her turtle said to her very slowly. "But we have to go outside," he said, and started to walk to the front door.

Sara got dressed, and followed the turtle. Outside her home, the turtle stopped. He looked at Sara and smiled.

"Watch this," he said. His shell started to grow...and grow...and grOW

It was as big as a car. And there was a door. The turtle opened the door. "Come in. It's quiet in here."

And every time Sara wanted to stay in a quiet place, she and her turtle went outside and into the giant shell.

Story 7

Happy Birthday

Yesterday, Meri had the most exciting day

ever in her whole life.

She woke up at 6am because something

was licking her face…it was a dog…her new

dog. Her dad was looking into her room from

the door. He said, "Happy birthday Meri." It was Meri's birthday.

She was now 8 years old. She washed her face, brushed her teeth for 3 minutes, then went downstairs.

She was hungry because she could smell something super crazy delicious… PANCAKES! Her favorite food was pancakes. Her mom made a stack of pancakes for Meri, and Meri ate them all.

They were unbelievably DEEEEEEEEEEEEEELICIOUS!!!!!

It was Saturday, so Meri had no school. Suddenly, somebody knocked on her door. Meri ran to the door, opened the door, and she saw…

Captain Krazyface, her favorite cartoon

character.

The captain said, "Arrr, today tis yee birthday. Yee is invited ta Pirateland. Bring ALL of your friends too."

Meri and all of her friends went to Pirateland, and had SO much fun. It was her best day EVER!

Story 8

Hooked

In the ocean, there was a smart little fish called Finny. Finny was a small fish with short straight hair. It was a small fish , but it was very fast.

One day, Finny was swimming when it saw something shiny in the water. Finny liked shiny things, so it went close to it. Just then, another fish came close to Finny. It was a big fish with a round tail and a long nose.

The big fish said to Finny, "Hey, I want that shiny thing. It's mine." The shiny thing looked nice, really nice...too nice.

Finny was a smart fish, and it knew that things that were too good sometimes weren't so good.

So, Finny told the big fish, "You know, I think you shouldn't...."

But the big fish got angry. "Are you telling me what to do?" asked the big fish.

"Well, no, but..." tried Finny, but the big fish took the shiny thing in its mouth.

Finny knew a fisherman was waiting above the water, but the big fish didn't know that. Finny swam away and never saw the big fish ever again.

Story 9

The Brave Goldfish

Aki lived with 2 friends in a bowl. Aki was a goldfish, and every day, a nice boy called Shuey put food into the bowl. It was the same food every day, but Aki thought it was delicious.

Then one day, Shuey got a new pet…a cat. Aki had never seen a cat before. He thought the cat was really big, and a little scary.

When Shuey went to school, the cat and the goldfish were alone. The cat walked slowly to the bowl. The cat was about to put its paw into the water when Aki shouted,

"S h h h h h h h h h h h h h h t o p !"

The cat asked, "Why did you yell at me?"

Aki didn't know why, but he was afraid of the cat.

"Because," said Aki, "if you touch the water, you will turn into a goldfish…like us. We were cats before, but when we touched this water…**POOF**!…we became goldfish."

The cat looked afraid.

"Thanks. I was going to eat you for a snack, but I don't want to be a fish."

After that, the cat and Aki were best

friends. And Aki was happy about that.

Story 10

Mystery

"Oh no," said Nana, "I can't find my socks."

Nana was 8 years old. She had long brown hair that was a little wavy, big brown eyes, and her favorite color was...purple.

"Sooooocks...where are you?" she shouted

outside her bedroom. Her mom and dad were eating breakfast. Nana was hungry, but she HAD to find her socks.

"Did you look on your feet?" her dad asked. Nana didn't answer. She never answered silly questions.

"Which socks are you looking for?" her mom asked. "The pink ones with the blue dots and yellow stars," Nana answered. "I saw them yester…"

Suddenly, Nana saw her cat Pooky running into the living room, and her socks were in its mouth.

"Pooooooooky," Nana yelled, and she started to chase her cat. But the cat was too fast, the cat was too quick, the cat would run past Nana, it wasn't a trick.

Nana had an idea. She got Pooky's favorite snack, PICKLES, and brought three pickles to the living room.

"Pooky, I'll trade you these pickles for my socks," said Nana.

Pooky stopped running, looked at her, and said, "That's a FANTASTIC idea," and the cat gave Nana her socks.

Story 11
The Wrong Pet

It was Toma's birthday, and he wanted a pet.

He asked his mom, "Mommy, can we have a

dog…or a cat…or a bird?" but his mom said

no.

Toma was allergic to those animals. But he didn't give up.

"Then what kind of pet can we have?" he asked his mom again.

She was cooking dinner, and was a little busy. "Well," she answered while cutting up some broccoli, "I guess a small lizard would be okay."

Toma ran out of the house. Yes, he thought, a lizard would be a great pet. He ran and ran and ran until he got to a river close to his home.

Toma lived in Australia. He took out his net, and threw it into the water. In 5 seconds, like magic, he caught a lizard.

He ran back home holding his lizard. The door flew open, Toma dashed into the kitchen.

"Mom, look," and he showed his new pet to his mom.

"Arrrrrrrr," she screamed. "Get that crocodile out of the house!!!"

Story 12

A Grape Story

Every year, there was a contest for young

children. The contest was very simple: who

could eat the most grapes in 2 minutes. Many

children love grapes, especially Emma. So,

she wanted to win the contest very very very

much.

The contest was at a farm, so Emma and her mom drove there. It was very far. It took 1 hour to go there.

Emma and her mom went into a building. There were many children there, and they all looked hungry. But Emma was hungry too. Emma and the children sat down at a table filled with grapes.

A man said, "On your mark, get set…. EAT!"

All the children started to eat the grapes. After 2 minutes, they all stopped. Emma ate 79 grapes, but the winner ate 203 grapes.

"Oh honey, you didn't win," Emma's mom said sadly. But Emma had a big smile on her face.

Emma didn't win the contest, but she wasn't sad. She ate 79 delicious grapes, so she was very happy about that.

Story 13
The Peach

It was a hot summer day, and Sam was very hungry. He asked his mom for something to eat. "Here is a peach," she said, "but put the seed in the garbage." Sam said yes, and took the peach.

It was the most delicious peach he ever ate.

It was juicy and soft and sweet. He ate it in 10 seconds, then threw the seed out his window.

The next morning, Sam was sleeping when he heard a sound. The sound was outside his window. He opened his window, and saw a giant peach tree.

But the peach tree was dancing, and Sam's house was shaking. The peach tree was very heavy and not very graceful. The branches on the tree hit Sam's house.

Just then, Sam's mom came out. She said, "Peach tree, go dance somewhere else."

The peach tree sadly left.

Then, Sam's mom yelled, " Saaaaaaaaaaaaaaaaam, come here RIGHT NOW!"

Sam was afraid. He didn't listen to his

mom. So, Sam decided to go back to sleep and stay in bed all day.

Story 14

The Apple

In Rere Park, there was a big apple tree.

Everyday, people came and picked the

delicious, red apples from the tree, including a

little boy called Ringi.

Ringi was a young boy who really, really,

really, really liked apples, but he had a small

problem.

He was short.

He couldn't get any apples. He just watched other people picking apples from the big tree.

One day, Ringi walked under the tree. At the top, he saw an incredibly big apple. It was so high, but he wanted it badly. He made a plan.

The next day, he went to the tree. The apple looked even more delicious than the day before.

He was wearing a coat, but it wasn't a normal coat: it was a bread coat. Ringi knew birds loved bread.

Suddenly, a lot of birds came to him. The birds started to eat his bread coat.

Then, Ringi screamed, "**Booboobooboo**,"
and the birds flew away. Ringi also put glue
on the bread coat, so the birds' legs stuck to it.

When the birds flew away, they carried
Ringi with them. Ringi was flying like a bird.

The birds flew right over the apple tree.

3, 2, 1...JUMP!

He jumped out of his coat and landed on
top of the tree. He got the apple.

Crrrrrrunch!

He bit into the apple. It was soooooooooooo
ooooooooooooooooooooooooooooooooooooooooo
delicious.

Ringi sat at the top of the tree, eating the
most delicious apple in the world.

But for Ringi, there was just one problem...

Story 15

Chaka

A long time ago, there was a dinosaur called
Chaka. Chaka was a small, green dinosaur,
and she liked to eat flowers. Her favorite
flowers were red and they smelled like

potatoes.

One day, Chaka was hungry, so she went outside to find some food. It was snowing outside, and she was a little cold. She walked to the river because the flowers grew there. At the river, she saw an old dinosaur taking a bath.

The old dinosaur said, "Hi Chaka, are you looking for something?" Chaka said yes.

"Me hungry, but me can,t see no my favorite flowers."

The old dinosaur said, "That's because it's winter. Flowers don't grow in winter. Do you want to try sashimi?"

"What,s sesame?" asked Chaka. The old dinosaur threw a piece of sushi right into Chaka's mouth.

GULP!

Chaka swallowed the sashimi, and it was sooooooo tasty.

Now, sashimi was her favorite food, but Chaka still liked to eat potato-smelling flowers...just not in winter.

Story 16
The Painter

Leo was a very good painter. He liked to paint clocks, socks and people taking a walk.

One day, he painted a bird, a beautiful blue bird with a yellow beak and big purple eyes. After he finished, Leo went to sleep.

In the morning, when he woke up, there

was something on his face. Yuck!

It was hairy…

It was a bird…

It was a blue bird with a yellow…

It was the bird he painted.

"Oh, you are awake. Good. Thank you for drawing me. I am hungry. I want to eat a few worms. You are a very good painter. Bye bye," and the bird flew out his window.

Leo was shocked. His painting became real. That day, he went to school fast, came home fast, finished his homework fast, and started to paint a new picture slowly.

It was a giant, hot, delicious pizza.

Leo went to sleep…thinking about the pizza he was going to eat for breakfast the next day…and the next day…and every day after that.

Leo decided to draw pizza every day.

Story 17
Ice Cream

Yura was walking to her home after school. It

was a hot day, and she wanted to eat some ice

cream. She walked into an ice cream store.

"Can I have an ice cream cone please? Strawberry," said Yura with a smile on her face.

"Sure...here you go," and the man gave Yura a strawberry ice cream cone. But he also gave her chocolate, vanilla, and miso ice cream. The ice cream cone was HUGE!

She gave the man 200 yen, and left the store. It was even hotter outside. Eating ice cream on hot days is great. But there is a problem.

She thought, 'I will wait and eat my ice cream at home.' Yura walked for 1 minute, and the ice cream was melting. 'Oh no,' she thought, 'I have to run,' and she started to run to her home.

Two minutes later, she got home, but the ice cream was like soup.

Her mom took the ice cream cone and told her, "Wash your hands. You are soooo messy." And the mom put the ice cream soup in the garbage.

Story 18
The Hole

Hara was walking in a forest, looking at birds and bees and apples and asparaguseses. Hara was 12 years old, and his house was close to the forest. His mom said, "Be careful in the forest. Always come home before dark."

Hara liked to climb trees. He looked like a monkey when he did this. He was walking and looking into the sky when suddenly he fell into a deep hole, **whooshhhh**. When Hara looked up, he saw a girl standing there.

"Ha, I caught a monkey," she said.

"I am not a monkey," he said angrily. The girl threw him a banana. "Thanks," he said. Hara loved bananas.

It was starting to get dark, but the girl kept throwing bananas to Hara. Suddenly, Hara heard his mom calling, "Haaaaaaaaaaaa Raaaaaaaaa."

The girl told Hara's mom he was in the hole.

"Again?" asked the mom.

Together, the mom and girl pulled Hara out

with a rope.

Hara was more careful in the forest after that.

Story 19

Watermelon Queen

Mugmug was a little girl who lived in a big house on top of a mountain. Her mom and dad were farmers. They grew the most delicious watermelons in the world. Even their house looked like a watermelon.

Everybody wanted to eat Mugmug's

watermelons. But, they were very expensive.

One day, a zebra came to Mugmug's house. The zebra said, "I am so hungry. Can I have a watermelon please?" Mugmug gave the zebra one watermelon.

The next day, a frog came to Mugmug's house. The frog said, "I love watermelons. Can I have 2 please?" Mugmug gave the frog 3 watermelons. She was kind.

The next day, a fox came and tried to steal all of Mugmug's watermelons. But the zebra saw the fox, and pushed him into a pond.

If the fox asked for a watermelon, MugMug would have given him one...or two...or maybe even three.

Mugmug's watermelons were safe, and they had a big watermelon party.

Story 20

The Girl Who Loved Broccoli

Menda hated broccoli. She thought they

looked like trees. But her mom loved broccoli.

Menda's mom put broccoli on toast, she

made broccoli pudding, and she even bought

broccoli toothpaste.

At school, Menda's friends also didn't like broccoli. One day, Menda forgot her lunch. She had no food to eat.

So she sat at the lunch table, watching her friends eat. "Arrrr," said one friend, "broccoli soup." She pushed the soup away. "Bllllah," said another friend, "broccoli sandwiches," and she pushed them away. And another said, "Harrrumph, broccoli ice cream," and didn't eat it.

Menda's stomach was making sounds... **Grrrrrrrr-whrrrrrrrrrrr-brrrrrrrrrrrrrrrrrr-BOING!**

She was crazy hungry. So, she asked her friends, "**Ummm**, well, can I try your..." and her friends pushed the soup, sandwiches and ice cream to her.

Slurp, crunch, lick, Menda ate the soup, sandwiches and ice cream. And she was surprised. They didn't taste like trees. They were...yummy.

So now, Menda loves broccoli, but she still doesn't like broccoli tooth paste. She likes carrot toothpaste more.

Story 21

The Sneezer

"AHHHHHHHHHH CHOOOOOOOOOOOOOOOO
OOOOOOOOOOOOOOOOOOOOO," blasted

Hugo in the library close to his home. One

person jumped, another person dropped 7

books, and another person screamed.

"AHHHHHHHHHHH Choooooo," Hugo

blasted again. He was sick. He caught a cold.

And for four days, he didn't stop sneezing. His mom told him to leave the house. He was really noisy, and she was tired of hearing "AH CHOO".

So, he went to the library. But people in the library were angry at him too. So, Hugo sat alone in the corner.

Suddenly, a robber came into the library. He had a gun. "Give me your money," he shouted, "NOW!" Hugo was the first person he walked to.

"Give me your..." the bad man started to say. But Hugo began to sneeze, a really big sneeze, maybe the biggest sneeze ever in the universe +1.

"AHHHHHHHHHHHHHHHHHHHHHHHHHHHH-
HHHHHHHHHHHHHHHHHHHHHHHHHHHHHHHH

CHOOOOOOOOOOOOOOOOOOOOOOOOOOOO
OOOOOOOOOOOOOOOOOOOOOOOOOOOO
OOOOOOOOOOOOOOOOOOOOOOOOOOOO
OOOOOOOOOOOOOOOOOOOOOOOO," Hugo

sneezed so strongly that his green monsters

hit the bad guy in the face, and knocked him

out.

K.O.!

Everybody in the library cheered. Hugo

was ah...ah...ah...hero.

Story 22

Winter Is Here

Ren was 6 years old, and she didn't like winter. She liked the snow, she liked the cold, but her mom didn't want her to go outside with her.

"It's too cold," her mom told her. "You shouldn't go outside today." So Ren watched her friends playing outside in the snow.

One day, there was a KNOCK-KNOCK on Ren's door. She opened it, and it was her friend Maki.

"Hi Ren," said Maki. "Do you want to make a snowman with me?" Maki asked. Ren's mom was making bread in the kitchen. "Well," said Ren quietly, looking behind to see if her mom was coming, "okay." She got dressed fast, and ran outside.

They made the snowman in front of Ren's home, and it was a giant snowman. It had rock eyes, a hotdog mouth, and 2 hockey stick arms...but it was missing one important part of its face.

The snowman had no nose.

Suddenly, Ren's mom came outside. "What

are you doing?" she asked. Ren was quiet.

"Your snowman," said Ren's mom,
"doesn't have a nose." She gave Ren a carrot.

Ren put the carrot into the snowman's
head.

The carrot was his nose.

"You have a delicious nose," Ren's mom
said. They all laughed...even the snowman.

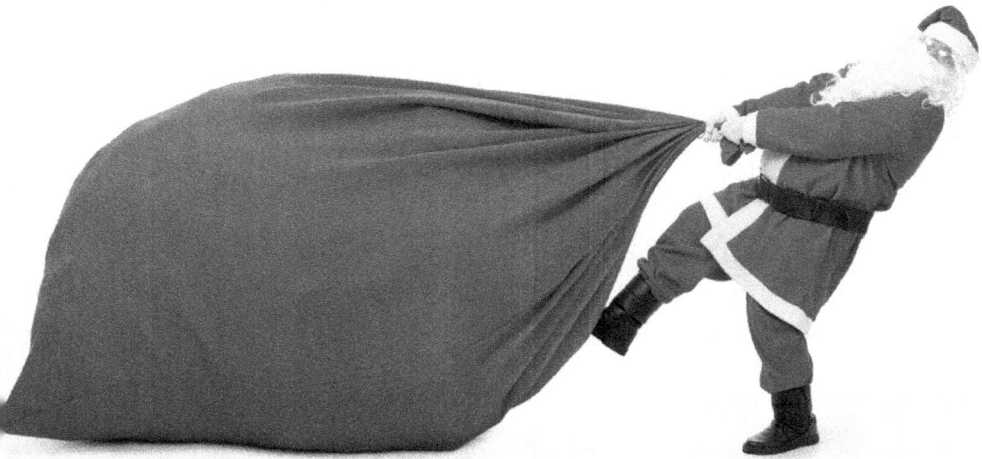

Story 23

Santa

It was Christmas Day, and Santa was ready.

He woke up at 4am. For breakfast he ate some

bread, a banana, and 3 pieces of bacon. He got

dressed fast, and went outside. He saw his

sleigh, but something wasn't right.

There were no presents inside the sleigh.

"Oh my," said Santa, "what will I do?"
All of Santa's presents were gone, and it was
Christmas Day.

Santa looked in his home, looked up in
the trees, looked under some rocks, searched
under the sea. Nothing.

Santa was sad, he started to cry, "What will
I do?" he looked to the sky. "I know," he said,
"I know what to do."

He ran through his house, grabbing
everything he saw. He took dolls and cups,
puzzles and balls.

Santa had a lot of great things in his house,
and he gave them all to the children in the
world.

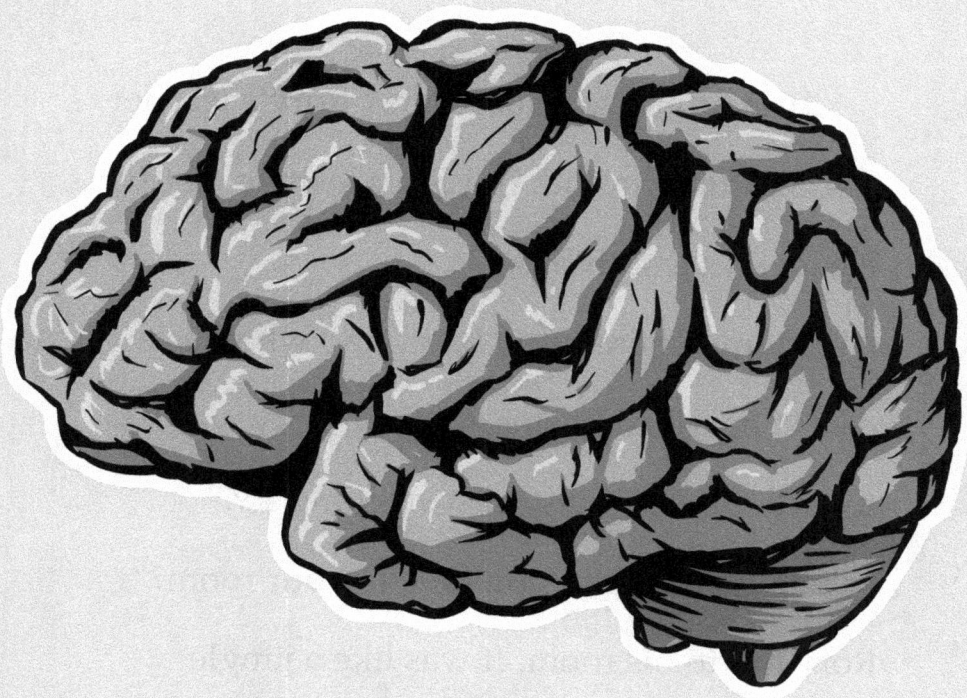

Story 24

Mom, Where Is My...

"Where is my bag?" Rory asked his mom.

He was a 7 year old boy with short black hair, a big smile, and no front teeth. His 2 front teeth fell out of his mouth at school. His friends thought it was AMAZING!

"Bring these to your mom," Rory's teacher Ms. Skuttlebutt said. But Rory lost the teeth. He always lost things.

"Mom, where is my bag…and where is my coat?" he asked his mom again. Rory was late for school. His mom was watching TV.

She asked, "Did you look in your room?" Rory ran to his room. It was like a jungle inside his room. Clothes and books and chairs and monkeys were EVERYWHERE.

Rory looked and looked, but didn't find his bag or coat or teeth.

"Mom, where is my homework…and bag, and coat…and how about my lunch for school?" Rory was looking everywhere in the jungle. He found an old banana, some bottles of shampoo, and a small TV. But no bag, no homework, no lunch.

"Mom, I am going to be late. Please help," Rory begged his mom.

"Late for what?" his mom asked, "today is Sunday."

Rory even forgot the days of the week.

Story 25

Stinky Socks

"Yuck, what's that smell," Mr. Bingbong asked his class.

All of the students looked at Kevin. The windows were closed. The door was closed. The smell was getting worse, and everyone knew it was Kevin.

He took off his shoes. Again.

Kevin was a 6 year old boy with short brown hair, a sharp nose, and really stinky feet. But this was strange because...

(1) He washed his feet three times a day with soap.

(2) He always wore 4 pairs of socks.

(3) He bought new shoes every month.

But still his feet smelled like wet, juicy garbage cooking under the hot sun.

Mr. Bingbong ran to a window, and pushed it open. All of the students followed him to the window. All of the windows were now open.

Suddenly, a wolf jumped through a window. It was a hungry, hairy scary wolf with big, sharp teeth.

It started to walk towards Kevin, but Kevin was smart. He took his shoe, put it to his mouth, and blew hard.

Whoooossshhhhhh.

A green gas from his shoe flew towards the wolf. The gas hit the wolf in the face.

The wolf started to choke, the wolf started to shake, the wolf started to turn green, and it jumped back out the window. Everybody cheered, "Hurray for Kevin!!!"

Kevin was a hero. Being stinky wasn't so bad after all.

Story 26
The Scary Lion

Shizi was the strongest lion in the jungle. He was big and loud and very scary. But he was not a kind animal. Shizi was not nice to the other animals in the jungle. So, other animals didn't like him and they were afraid of him.

Why didn't the animals like Shizi? Because Shizi took grapes from the giraffes…**chomp-chomp-ROAR**.

He drank the zebras' water…gulp-gulp.

Shizi slept in the baboons' bed…**zzzzzzz-chomp-ROAR**.

He even went to the bathroom in the hippos' pond…**psssssss-ROAR**-YUCK!

Shizi had no friends, and every animal didn't like him.

One day, the lion was walking in the jungle. It was hot and cloudy.

Suddenly, a net landed on Shizi. It was a hunter. "ROOOOAAAARRRR," screamed Shizi. "Help me…"

But nobody helped Shizi.

The hunter dragged Shizi to his super-strong truck, and put Shizi inside a cage.

"NOOOOOOOOOOO..." roared Shizi.

Shizi was put in a zoo. But life wasn't so bad for Shizi the mean lion.

He got food every day.

He never had to hunt.

He had a nice bed.

After some time, Shizi was even happier than before. And so were the animals in the jungle.

Story 27

The Cookie Monster

"I love cookies," said Anna to her mom,

"especially oatmeal cookies." Anna's mom

was in the kitchen, baking something.

Today was Anna's birthday. She was 7

years old, and she really really really wanted to eat oatmeal cookies…and pizza…and cake. Anna liked food, but she wasn't fat. She was tall and strong because she also ate vegetables like carrots and asparagus.

"**Brrring…brrring…**" Anna's mom's phone rang.

"Hello,' said her mom. "Okay, I will go now." Anna's mom had to go outside for 10 minutes.

After 10 minutes, she came back. But Anna was on the ground, holding her stomach, smiling.

"Mom," she said, "something bad happened. Something horrible. Something incredible. A cookie monster went into the kitchen and ate 11 super-yummy oatmeal cookies with a glass of cold milk. Can you make more?"

Anna's mom stared at Anna, and began to laugh.

"Sure...cookie monster," and she started baking more cookies.

Story 28

Fire Butt

Mac liked to eat spicy food. He loved curry

for breakfast, he put Tabasco sauce in his

coffee, and he even had hot pepper shampoo.

Mac loved hot things.

Mac's job was a fireman, but he was not such a good fireman. Mac didn't want to put out fires. He wanted the fires to burn and burn and burn. In fact, he was a terrible fireman.

One day, Mac was working. "**Brrrrring Brrrring**" rang the fire bell. There was a fire in the city. "Hurry up Mac," said Mac's boss. All the firemen jumped into the fire truck. But the truck didn't move. It was broken.

"Oh no!" said the fire chief. "What can we do?"

Mac got an idea. He said, "Let me try something." He walked to the back of the fire truck.

"I will use my **errrrrrr** natural gas

mmmmmmmm power to **arrrrrrrr**…" and

Mac pushed and pushed.

Mac's face was red. "Hold on!" shouted

Mac.

BUUUUUUUUUUUUUUUUUUUUUUU

UUUUUUUUUUUUUUUUUUUUUUUUU

UUUUUUUUUUU.

Mac's pants ripped, fire came out his

butt, and the fire truck flew in the air to the

building on fire.

The firemen put out the fire, and Mac was a

hero with no pants.

Story 29

The Hungry Boy

Nick's parents were always busy, always

working. This made Nick sad because they

didn't cook food for him. Nick cooked his own food. But there was a problem.

He was not a good cook.

He ate bread and cheese every day. He was always hungry, and he was always tired. He usually fell asleep doing homework.

"Ohhhh, I am soooo hungry," he told his friend Toko.

"Would you like to come to my house?" Toko asked. "My mom's a great cook."

At Toko's home, Nick ate fantastic french fries. He ate amazing asparagus. He drank delicious dragon juice. "Here is the best food of all," said Toko's mom. "An apple."

Toko's mom gave Nick a big, green apple.
Nick said thank you and went home. But he
didn't eat the apple.

'It is so delicious…I will keep it,' Nick
thought. One week…two weeks…three
weeks…he didn't eat the apple. 'No, I
can't eat the apple,' Nick thought. 'It is too
delicious.'

After 1 year, Nick was so hungry, so he
decided to eat the apple…but it was rotten.

Nick started to cry. He never got the chance
to eat the delicious green apple.

Story 30

The Fisherman

One day, a group of fishermen had a contest. They

wanted to know who the best fisherman was. The person

who caught the biggest fish won a prize, and it was a

GREAT prize: A gold coin. All of the fishermen were

excited, especially Marco. He really wanted to win the

gold coin, so he made a plan.

It was a cold, wet morning, and the contest began. Marco was fishing in his favorite spot, and he caught a big, yellow fish. 'No,' he thought, 'I want bigger.'

After 1 hour, he caught a big red fish. 'No,' he thought again, 'I want bigger.' After 3 hours, he caught a very big green fish. 'No,' he thought again, 'I want bigger.' Marco fished and fished, trying to catch the supermostbiggestgiantest fish ever.

But the contest finished, and Marco wasn't the winner. He didn't catch any more fish. But Marco didn't stop.

"I won't give up," he said.

Nobody ever saw Marco again. Many people believe he is still fishing. Looking for the biggest fish.

Thanks for the visit

QuESTiONS

(1) Greedy

1. What was Tom's problem?
2. What was the store's name?
3. What did Tom eat in the store?
4. Who was angry at Tom?
5. Where was Tom's mom waiting for him?
6. Did Tom buy the potato chips?

(2) The Girl and Her Cow

1. Where did Rena live?
2. What did she want for her birthday?
3. What kind of food did Rena love?
4. When did Rena go to the cow?
5. Where did Rena put the cow?

(3) Fall

1. What colors did the leaves change into?
2. What is Suzi's favorite season?
3. What does Suzi do in Fall?
4. How does Suzi go into the pile of leaves?
5. Why can't she play with the leaves anymore?
6. Do you think Suzi likes winter?

QuESTiONS

(4) Always Late

1. Why was Tony's teacher angry?
2. What did Tony step on?
3. What did the turtle wear?
4. What did Tony buy?
5. Was he late again for school?

(5) Moon Boy

1. What mountain did they want to climb?
2. Was it a small mountain?
3. How was the air?
4. Why does Sam want to live on the moon?
5. How many people live on the moon?

(6) The Turtle and the Airport

1. Why was Sara's house noisy?
2. What was louder than the turtle?
3. How many brothers & sisters did Sara have?
4. How big did the shell grow?
5. How did the turtle speak?
6. Was it loud inside the shell?

QuESTiONS

(7) Happy Birthday

1. What time did Meri wake-up?
2. How old is she?
3. How long did she brush her teeth?
4. How many pancakes did she eat?
5. What day was it?
6. What present did her dad give her?

(8) Hooked

1. What kind of fish was Finny?
2. What did Finny see in the water?
3. Did the big fish have a square tail?
4. Who was waiting above the water?
5. Where did Finny live?
6. Did Finny see the big fish again?

(9) The Brave Goldfish

1. How many goldfish lived in the bowl?
2. Did Aki eat different food every day?
3. What was the boy's name: Haty, Socky, or Shuey?
4. What did Aki tell the cat not to do?
5. What did the water do to cats?

QuESTioNS

(10) Mystery

1. What colour were Nana's eyes?
2. What question did Nana's dad ask her?
3. What were Nana's mom & dad doing?
4. What was pooky's favourite snack?
5. What kind of socks was Nana looking for?
6. Was Pooky a slow runner?

(11) The Wrong Pet

1. Why was the day a special day?
2. What kind of pet did Toma want?
3. Why couldn't he have those pets?
4. Where did Toma live?
5. Where did he find the lizard?
6. Why did his mom scream?

(12) A Grape Story

1. What kind of contest did Emma want to win?
2. Where was the contest?
3. How did they go there?
4. How long did it take to go there?
5. Was Emma hungry?
6. How many grapes did she eat?
7. Was Emma sad about not winning? If no, why not?

QuESTiONS

(13) The Peach

1. What fruit did Sam eat?
2. Where did his mom tell him to put the seed?
3. How did the peach taste?
4. In the morning, what was the peach tree doing?
5. Was the peach tree light?
6. Why did Sam go back to bed?

(14) The Apple

1. What color were the apples?
2. Why couldn't Ringi get the apples?
3. What did he say to make the birds fly away?
4. Where was the delicious apple?
5. What kind of coat did he have?
6. What do you think his problem was?

(15) Chaka

1. When did Chaka live?
2. What color was she?
3. What did her favorite flower smell like?
4. Where did the flowers grow?
5. What was the old dinosaur doing at the river?
6. Now, what is Chaka's favorite food?

QuESTiONS

(16) The Painter

1. What did Leo like to paint?
2. What color were the bird's eyes?
3. Where was the bird sitting?
4. Was the bird hungry?
5. What did the bird want to eat?
6. That night, what did Leo paint?

(17) Ice Cream

1. Where was Yura going?
2. What kind of ice cream does she like?
3. How much did the ice cream cost?
4. Why did Yura start to run?
5. When she got home, how was the ice cream?
6. What did her mom tell her to do?
7. Where did Yura's mom put the ice cream?

(18) The Hole

1. How did Hara's mom get him out of the hole?
2. What did Hara like to see in the forest?
3. What did Hara's mom tell him to always do?
4. Where was Hara's house?
5. What animal did Hara look like?
6. What kind of hole did he fall into?

QuESTiONS

(19) Watermelon Queen

1. Where did Mugmug live?
2. What kind of fruit did Mugmug's family grow?
3. How many watermelons did Mugmug give the frog?
4. What did the fox want to do?
5. Where did the zebra and frog push the fox?
6. What kind of party did they have?

(20) The Girl Who Loved Broccoli

1. What did Menda think broccoli looked like?
2. How many of Menda's friends liked broccoli?
3. Did Menda always bring her lunch to school?
4. What didn't Menda's friends eat?
5. What kind of toothpaste does Menda like?
6. Does Menda think broccoli is delicious now?

(21) The Sneezer

1. Where did Hugo go?
2. How long did he have a cold?
3. How many books did 1 person drop?
4. What is the name of the song?
5. How did Ami feel after hearing the song?
6. What did they eat for lunch?

QuESTiONS

(22) Winter Is Here

1. How old is Ren?
2. Why doesn't her mom want her to go outside?
3. What did Maki ask Ren to do?
4. What kind of eyes did the snowman have?
5. What didn't the snowman have?
6. Do you think the snowman's nose tasted bad?

(23) Santa

1. What time did Santa get up?
2. What was wrong with Santa?
3. What did he eat for breakfast?
4. Did Santa look for the presents in the sea?
5. How did Santa fix the problem?
6. Who did Santa give presents to?

(24) Mom, Where Is My...

1. What is Rory missing in his mouth?
2. Where did he lose his teeth?
3. What was Rory looking for?
4. What was his mom doing?
5. What did Rory's room look like?
6. What day was it?

QUESTIONS

(25) The Stinky Socks

1. How old was Kevin?
2. What did his feet smell like?
3. How often did he wash his feet?
4. What animal jumped into the class?
5. How did Kevin save everyone?
6. What colour was his foot gas?

(26) The Scary Lion

1. Where did Shizi live?
2. How many friends did he have?
3. Where did he sleep at night?
4. What did he do to the giraffes?
5. What did the hunter throw on Shizi?
6. Is Shizi sad or happy now?

(27) The Cookie Monster

1. How old was Anna?
2. Was Anna short?
3. How long did Anna's mom go outside?
4. What 3 things did Anna want to eat?
5. Was her mom angry?
6. Who do you think really ate the cookies?

QuESTioNs

(28) Fire Butt

1. What did Mac eat for breakfast?
2. What was his job?
3. Was he a bad fireman?
4. What happened to the fire truck?
5. What was on fire?
6. What color did Mac's face turn?

(29) The Hungry Boy

1. Why didn't Nick's parents cook?
2. What kind of cook was Nick?
3. What did Nick eat every day?
4. What was Nick's friend's name?
5. What did Nick eat at Toko's house?
6. Why didn't Nick eat the green apple?

(30) The Fisherman

1. What kind of contest did they have?
2. What was the prize?
3. How was the weather?
4. What colors were the fish he caught?
5. What is Marco probably doing right now?
6. Do you like to go fishing?

www.ingramcontent.com/pod-product-compliance
Lightning Source LLC
Chambersburg PA
CBHW070529030426
42337CB00016B/2165